A SCENT FROM THE ROSE OF SHARON

I0164549

A SCENT FROM THE ROSE OF SHARON

by *POWilson*

The Arts Forum, NYC

taf
NYC

The Arts Forum, NYC
Brooklyn, New York
www.theartsforum.com

© 2015 Patrick Owen Wilson
ISBN   978-0-9726429-5-8

Elizabeth Jo (Doyle) Wilson

Contents

- *and*

hands clenching, unclenched
thought sure then sand

things moving away
as the heart of hearts
that does not beat or breathe
but sings…
sings

we see the moon's reflection on the water
yet swear there is no moon,
the moon bears witness
yet we swear there is no sun

here in I, a candle
lit by two candles touching

always the same flame passed

before the candles
burn away

- *what Abram didn't know*

Sarah woke to a beam of sunlight
thru a window
from across the field,
it fell on her eyelids
and opened them

she rose quietly
with unaltered breath,
walked to the window
and looked down

in the yard there was a man
leading a horse out of the barn

she had taught him to lead the horse
and the horse to follow,
and the man to think
it was of his own design

- *from then*

she was partly fawn
and partly from her father's times
with her grandmother's words
sounding in her head
like African drums

you are more than something given,
she said

and the tide comes in,
and the lungs breathe long
and I, in the quiet evening's dim light
remember when
her warmth washed through my everything
like the tide over sand
with only a word
or the touch of her hand
like sunlight baths a garden,
like the senses warmed by a new thought

and at times, these more recent times
seem only an echo
from her and then

- *mother's broken things*

she sailed on rough waters gently

he stirred calm water without reason,
lunging at the beast not seen
who stole his father's face
and broke his mother's cherished things

with her own hand he broke them
flailing at words,
innuendo perceived,
he fights the great battle, he must
but the beast is not with him now

so he stirs these waters on his own...

one day a bus drove by
as he waited to cross,
and history was only that

the path he walked only his,
even if, he could not imagine,
even if, no one knew

the beast
the faceless father

and mother's broken things

- interior gnomes

and Elizabeth had six children
and each of them
inside their heads,
a little laughing gnome

and though it had been a long time...
still, the gnomes were laughing
and in some of them, angry
and in all of them, some of the time

and this is the way of the interior gnomes
passed down through the generations,
laughing, sometimes angry,

goading the host

- *from a mother's breath*

is it longing I see in the air around you?
you have been my warm sun on a cool day
and I wonder,
what is your warm sun

I still see water sparkling
splashed by infant hands,
and the warmth that only comes
from a mother's breath

you are to me that life of honesty,
like a tree is a tree,
transient and beautiful,

did you know that when your eyes open
it is for me the sun,
did you know your gentle laughter
is my religion

- *the very next thing*

what good is my voice if you can't hear it?
what good are these words if not for you?

the world has been frozen
arctic air silent and motionless
the last tree fallen,
my voice hollow
throat still
my queen confessor breathed in
and I stand here waiting
please
please breathe again

all clamor has ceased
and there is only the echo
of what once was,
what I still want to be

my sweet traveler
I can only bear to let you go,
I cannot imagine
the very next thing

- *aground*

within a cloud
black with rain
my hands turned numb,
weathered eyes turned down

all, it seems
is laced with tragedy,
and even the brightest things
turn to carbon,
this coal mind hidden
within a cloud
black with rain
and all turned down,
all dark and still
my will
aground

- *promenade*

mother, I see waves of people,
it is hard to focus in,
I see waves flowing out
into buildings and back again,
and the water washes down
through a dried creek bed,
all that has ever been,
the many so many
and I am one of them

today the string quartet plays Pachelbel,
today the sun shines
across the long blowing grass on the hill

because of you I love art and science
hard work and honesty
and people who talk in a sullen tone,
because of you
quiet nights on the divan
with a book,
because of you I chastise pride
and admire gentleness

today
looking down the road
through the tree's long curving tunnel of shade
where the squirrels run freely
and the sound of Bach's six French suites
play your promenade,
always, today

- *the water and the well*

music alone shall live
are the words to the round,
dancing in the magic air
sung sweetly
in the evening's amber hue,
led by you,
where art and artisans, alive and well,
call the tune,
the sound, the taste and smell,
good will and fare-thee-well,
into the sparkling sky
towards dawn,
I hear you playing the piano there
where the foyer light still shines,
like a fire in the wilderness,
where children sing
and players dwell,
the beacon of my heart's desiring,
the water and the well

- *my angel*

you stood strong
for things I cower from,
with your words rebuked
and your small frame battered,
eyes watered,
squinted, straight and steady

my father said
only the strong survive
before he learned
you were the strongest

I learned from you
there must be things we will not say,
lines a person will not cross,
you stood strong
where men in yellow rain coats winced,
where kings and warriors fought the wars,
there was no king to fight yours
and mother you stood strong
and loved the studious,
the stoic and humble,
the sturdy prince who declined the battle
and yet stood strong

my angel heroin

- *rise*

rise mother rise
bring your birthing ways back,
turn your warm summer gaze
to these black winter branches,
send out your words made of candor
to these cold words suspended,
bring back
the better days
that in these days seem ended

- a scent from the Rose of Sharon

it was your voice that called me here
sweet summer dancing
a scent from the Rose of Sharon,
your voice and the cool night shadow
where blessed days were spent
from one into the other,
and I did not know
the days were numbered…
the wisp and lilting pretty ones

and now so long past, it blows again
that same strong wind of summer
and with the wind, the one who left

I do not know what called me then,
the trees were dark
the clouds were threatening
my eyes were heavy
and my brain was tight
and could not turn,
and the distance called
and it seemed inevitable
in the sweet summer dancing…
a scent from the Rose of Sharon

- *a landscape painting*

one night
sunset to sunrise
a poet writes an epic,
all things moving and unmoved,
then ten, twelve, or twenty years are spent
on a single phrase...
what was the first not moved
moving thing

a door reopens
like a leaf falls from a tree
without hesitation
and, if there is a reason
none is perceived

at seventeen
a girl sees life stretched out before her
like a landscape painting
then once more
while looking back
at eighty-nine
or ninety-three

- *late November*

there is a black iron structure
behind the barely standing barn,
a machine once used, broken and left
one evening in late November
like a skeleton frozen erect
mid-step on a walk to the field

I stood there one night as a child,
my hand on cold metal,
looking out into the darkness

and I did not want anything
or think anything
or say anything
or wonder why nothing was said

and the time was still, air sweet
and the moon was perfect
one night, late November

- *vigil*

let us say love with a deep voice

and invoke our hearts with compliments,
yet not so far
as to cover your eyes

the air is filled and felt,
our hearts suspended,
breath chaste

let all be of you, as it is
here, where love is known
and cannot be mistaken

we are waiting,
and for what?

for the sky to open,
for the heart to break,
for the clouds to move away
yet linger

let's bring in the memory of ancestors

like the cultures that praise the earth

waiting in silence
for low resounding drums,
quietly,
remembering your tenderness

- *to the last blade of grass*

happy life
proud life,
tender words
so seldom spoken

save the children
as best you can

pioneer women,
carnival men

in a time when all moves
to the tune of when

another drum
and back again

the clarinet
slowly bent
in warm July
before the rain,
classical new world claims

mother, father
woman, man

all with love
to the last blade of grass

www.ingramcontent.com/pod-product-compliance
Lightning Source LLC
Chambersburg PA
CBHW060549030426
42337CB00021B/4511